Contents

The River Ganges is the Holy River of India. People visit it to say prayers. Many Hindus hope that when they die, the ashes of their burnt body will be thrown into the river.

sm

rtney

CAMBRIDGE
UNIVERSITY PRESS

PUBLISHED BY THE PRESS SYNDICATE OF THE UNIVERSITY OF CAMBRIDGE
The Pitt Building, Trumpington Street, Cambridge, United Kingdom

CAMBRIDGE UNIVERSITY PRESS
The Edinburgh Building, Cambridge CB2 2RU, UK
40 West 20th Street, New York, NY 10011–4211, USA
477 Williamstown Road, Port Melbourne, VIC 3207, Australia
Ruiz de Alarcón 13, 28014 Madrid, Spain
Dock House, The Waterfront, Cape Town 8001, South Africa

http://www.cambridge.edu.au

First published in 2004

Printed in Australia by Hyde Park Press

Typeface Plantin Light 14/17 pt *System* QuarkXPress® [PC]

National Library of Australia Cataloguing in Publication data
Hartney, Chris.
Hinduism.
For teenagers with reading ages below eleven.
ISBN 0 521 60111 8.
1. Hinduism — Juvenile literature. I. Title.
(Series: Livewire investigates [Cambridge]).
294.5

ISBN 0 521 60111 8 paperback

Acknowledgements:
Photographs: Cover and p. iv: Fredrik Renander: www. worldsphotos.com;
p. 8 AAP Image; p. 16 K.L.Kamat; p. 21 Ronald Fruin.

1 The Oldest Religion

Hinduism is a very old religion. Some people say that it is at least 6000 years old. There are a lot of gods in Hinduism. In fact, some believe there are many thousands.

A person who follows this religion is called a 'Hindu'. A Hindu might have a special god they pray to, but they still respect all of the other gods.

Some gods help people to be healthy and other gods help people get things done in their life.

People who follow Hinduism pray to the gods that they think can help them the most. They also pray to those gods that they like the best.

Some people say that all of these gods are just different faces of the one Great God.

Hinduism began in India. It is a religion closely connected to the mountains, rivers, villages and people of India. Hinduism can be found everywhere in the world that Indians live. Hindus welcome everyone into their temples.

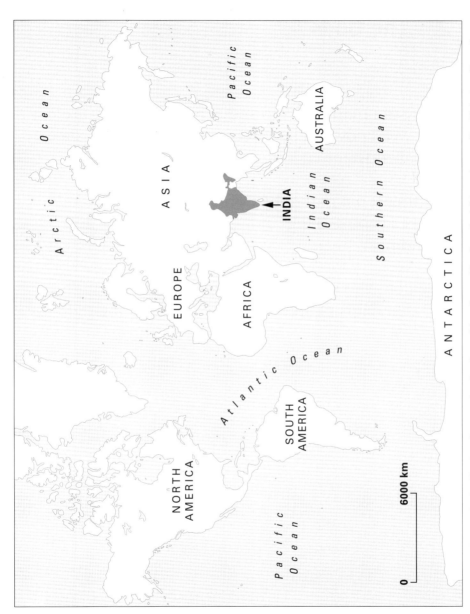

Hinduism began in India, but it can also be found in places like South Africa, Australia, Britain, Canada, Singapore and Fiji.

2 The Gods

There are many gods in India, but only a few are very well known. The three most important gods are called Brahma, Vishnu and Shiva.

Brahma is the god of beginnings, Vishnu is the god of keeping things going and Shiva is the god of endings.

The god who started life is Brahma. He is also the god that helps people start new things in their life.

Vishnu has a large number of followers and many temples all around India. He is the god that protects people. Vishnu also 'sustains' all that is good in the world – that means he keeps things going.

Vishnu makes sure the planets and stars are all right. He is famous for defeating bad spirits who try to hurt the world. He is also famous for coming down to Earth in the bodies of different people.

Hindus believe that Vishnu has appeared on Earth nine times already. They are waiting for him to come a tenth time.

Krishna is the lovable blue god of Hinduism. Many say he is the god Vishnu in a different body. Groups like the Hari Krishnas sing songs to him every day.

Hindus believe that Vishnu has already appeared on Earth as Buddha. Buddha began the religion called 'Buddhism'. Many people also believe that Vishnu appeared on Earth as another god called Krishna.

Krishna is a very playful and lovable god. He is blue. Krishna is the favourite god of many people. They love him so much that they sing songs to him many times each day.

Like Vishnu, Shiva also has a large following. He is often pictured with three eyes. His third eye appears in the middle of his forehead. It is always shut. People say that when Shiva opens this eye he can destroy everything.

Shiva is often shown dancing. He reminds people that the world and everything in it is always moving.

Shiva does not appear on Earth in the way Vishnu does. Instead, he is the father of a family of gods. His sons are very famous.

Ganesh is one of the sons of Shiva. Soon after Ganesh was born, his father accidentally destroyed his son's head. Shiva grabbed another head to fix his son.

The first thing Shiva picked up was the head of an elephant! He put this head on his son. This is why Ganesh has the head of an elephant but the body of a human.

Lots of people pray to Ganesh. He helps people get the other gods to listen to their prayers.

In India, everyone prays to Ganesh. He helps people to get the gods to listen to their prayers.

Ganesh loves to laugh. To get Ganesh to see them, Hindus will sometimes hit themselves on the head and pull their ears. They think this makes Ganesh laugh, so he is more likely to help the person who does this.

3 The Eternal Law

Religions answer big questions like, 'Why am I here?' and 'Why am I not as happy as other people?' Hindus answer these questions in a very special way.

Hindus call their answers the 'Eternal Law'. It is called 'eternal' because it lasts forever and never changes. For Hindus, this law explains everything.

The first part of the law says that we all have a soul. A soul is a holy part of us that we cannot see. It is the part of us that is most like the gods. It is our 'real' self.

When we are born, our soul is attached to our mind and our body. Hindus believe that when we die, our mind and our body die, but our soul keeps living. The soul never dies.

So where does the soul go when our body dies? Some religions say that our soul goes to heaven if we are good, or hell if we are bad.

Hindus think that after we die, our soul becomes attached to another body and another mind. We live again and again through many different lifetimes. This is called 'reincarnation'.

Hindus believe that the life we are living now is just one of thousands of lives that we have already lived. If we have been good, we are born into a new life that is better than our last life. If we have been bad, we are born into a worse life.

Hindus say this is true, not only for humans, but also for animals. A very bad human can be reborn as an animal. A very good animal can be reborn as a human.

4 The Groups of India

In India, there are many different social groups of people. This is called the 'caste system'. People are born into their caste. Each caste has a specific duty in society.

The people in one group might only run shops. The people in another group might be warriors such as policemen or soldiers, and in another group, priests.

If you are born into one of these castes, Hindus believe it is because of things you did in your last life.

Brahmins are the group of priests in India. They are the highest caste and are very important for running temples and helping people pray to the gods.

Hindus believe that if you are born into a poor group that has to do a lot of hard labour, this is because you did bad things in your last life.

If you are born into a rich and powerful group, it is because you were very good in your last life and you are being rewarded.

The highest of all of these groups are the priests. The priests are called 'Brahmins'.

At Hindu temples, only men born into the
Brahmin caste can say special prayers and present
gifts to the gods.

Brahmins use a special language called 'Sanskrit'
to do this. This language is so old that almost
no one speaks it except for the priests.

Many people in India hope to be reborn into the
group of priests. They do good things for other
people and ask the gods to help them to do this.

5 The Home and the Temple

Hinduism is important in the home. Sometimes statues of the gods are placed around the home and in the car to help keep people safe.

Hindus believe that people should take care of each other and that family is a holy thing. A husband and wife should treat each other kindly.

People offer the gods prayers so that children will grow up healthy and good in their studies.

Temples are places where important statues of the gods are placed. They are also decorated with many other things. These all help remind Hindus of the importance of the gods.

The temple is a very good place to say prayers and a good place to brings gifts for the gods.

Most temples also have priests. Each morning a priest will wake up and go to the temple. The first thing they do is wash the statues of the gods and dress them in new clothes for the day.

Temples are very lovely places were people can come and pray to the gods. Many temples have large, beautiful towers over their doors. These towers can be seen from a long way off to remind people to think of the gods as they approach.

Hindus go to the temple at any time, but Friday is a very good day to go. Before leaving their homes, Hindus wash and put on nice clothes.

When they get to the temple, they go to the desk of the temple keeper. There they can buy gifts to give to the gods. Fruit and flowers are the main gifts people give.

To give their gift, people ask the priest to take their offerings before their special god. The priest is trained to say special prayers. As the priest prays, they also say the name of the person who is giving the gift.

The priest will also light a lamp and hold it in front of the face of the god. This is so that the person giving the gift can see the face of the god.

When the prayers are over, the priest will sometimes give the person a little piece of sugar. This is to remind the giver of the gift how sweet the help of the god can be.

Sometimes people will ask the priest to wash the god again for them. The priest will say prayers and pour milk, spices and other lovely things over the statue of the god. Hindus hope that this will please the god.

6 Holy Writings

'Scriptures' are the holy books of a religion.
In Hinduism, there are more scriptures than
in any other religion.

The oldest scripture in Hinduism is called the
'Rg-Veda' (this is said Rig-Vay-der). This is a
collection of very old prayers written in the
language of Sanskrit. All of its prayers start with
the special sound: 'OM'. Hindus believe that this
was the sound that was made when the world was
created.

Many scriptures answer questions about life.
Others scriptures deal with the gods. Many of
these scriptures tell very clever stories.

One of these great stories can be found in a poem called the 'Mahbharata'. This is the longest poem in the world. It tells the story of two royal families that fought each other.

One small part of this large poem has its own name: it is called the 'Bhagavad-Gita'. In this part, the warrior-hero called Arjuna gets ready for a war.

Arjuna rides into the space between two great armies as they get ready to attack each other. He looks over at the enemy and sees many people he grew up with. He hates the idea of killing them. Suddenly he does not want to fight. Close to him is a servant who is actually the god Krishna. The god talks to Arjuna.

Krishna tells Arjuna that because he was born into the warrior group, he must fight. It is his duty. Krishna also tells Arjuna that even if he dies in the battle, he will be born again. Death is just a door into the next life.

It is a really good story and the cleverness of Arjuna and Krishna make the Bhagavad-Gita one of the most famous scriptures in India.

7   Hinduism Today

About 300 years ago, the British invaded India and took control of it. The British were Christians.

At first, the British did not like Hinduism. They tried to make the people of India into Christians. But the more the British understood Hinduism, the more they realised how old and great this religion was.

After India became part of the British Empire, wherever the British went, Hindus also settled. This is why there are lots of Hindus today in Africa, the West Indies and Fiji. Many Hindus also migrated to the United States, Canada and Australia.

The British stopped controlling India about 50 years ago. Since then, Hinduism has become stronger. Hinduism is the heart of India.

Its Eternal Law has also helped other religions develop, like Buddhism.